color me slimmer

color me slimmer

clever dressing for a fabulous figure

colour**me**beautiful

the image consultants

Pat Henshaw
Veronique Henderson

hamlyn

An Hachette UK Company
www.hachette.co.uk

First published in Great Britain in 2010 by Hamlyn,
a division of Octopus Publishing Group Ltd
Endeavour House
189 Shaftesbury Avenue
London
WC2H 8JY
www.octopusbooks.co.uk

Distributed in the USA and Canada for Octopus Books USA
by Hachette Book Group USA
237 Park Avenue
New York, NY 10017

ISBN-13 978-0-600-62162-1

Printed and bound in China

10 9 8 7 6 5 4 3 2 1

Contents

Introduction

There comes a time in many a woman's life when she wishes she could look and feel a little slimmer. The advice given here is for every woman, whatever her size or age, to help her to gain the confidence to dress with style and flair, while making the most of the attributes that nature has given her. Our world is full of women of all shapes and sizes, and fabulous for it, too!

For three decades, **colour me beautiful** consultants (who also come in all shapes and sizes) have shared their knowledge with millions of clients worldwide. In doing so, we have helped countless women achieve confidence in how they present themselves to others. The feedback we receive is proof that we have given many women a new lease of life.

Celebrity culture has made many women with a dress size in the teens or twenties feel that their bodies are unacceptable. And yet there are celebrities who make fantastic role models, dressing with panache, glamour, and elegance. These women have learned to make the most of their bodies. It is all a question of understanding your body, and acknowledging the parts that you do like as well as those that you don't.

Finding the new you

This book will show you that you can achieve a slimmer look by buying the right clothes for your body shape. Of course, this is fundamental, but there are other things to consider as well. You may be surprised to discover that your natural coloring—hair,

skin tone, eyes—can play a significant role when it comes to looking slimmer, specifically by wearing colors that enhance such features. Careful grooming and accessorizing also have a place, completing the image of a well-dressed, confident woman.

Not all of us fit exactly into neat little boxes, for each one of us is different in many subtle ways. But be in no doubt that this book will help you to develop a better understanding of your body and the types of clothes and accessories that complement your shape and coloring. Your wardrobe will definitely change! And for those readers who want to take their slimmer look one step further, why not take this opportunity to visit a **colour me beautiful** image consultant for personal advice that is relevant to you and you alone.

RIGHT Jessica Simpson (Soft), Queen Latifah (Deep), and Adele (Warm) show how choosing the right colors can result in striking and flattering looks.

Introducing the models

We have chosen nine models to help illustrate our philosophy. They range in shape and size, but also in their natural coloring. Each of them appears throughout the book, showing how best to dress for her figure.

Our models

We have chosen our models carefully, in the hope that they will not only help you to discover how to make the most of your figure but inspire you to try some of the tips and advice within these pages. You can see that they are different ages, coloring and build.

For some of you, it will be a matter of discovering how to dress your shape, others will find that their proportions might be the challenge, and some their bone structure. Don't worry if you find you are a little of one thing and a bit of another—this is normal as we are all unique. Finding out what is special about you is what counts.

Mel
SHAPE: Curvy top and bottom
COLORING: Light

Laura
SHAPE: Narrow shoulders, full hips
COLORING: Clear

Nina
SHAPE: Very curvy, short waist
COLORING: Soft

Amy
SHAPE: Straight top, curvy bottom
COLORING: Warm

Emma
SHAPE: Straight top and bottom
COLORING: Deep

Christie
SHAPE: Curvy top and bottom,
grand scale
COLORING: Deep

Veronique
SHAPE: Curvy top, straight bottom
COLORING: Cool

Lisa
SHAPE: Curvy top and bottom,
petite in height
COLORING: Deep

Sarah
SHAPE: Curvy top and bottom
COLORING: Soft

slimmer body

A positive image

Before you change your wardrobe you need to be comfortable with your body image—this means accepting your body shape and making the most of the way you look and feel.

A clear vision

The first step to a positive image is to be completely honest about how you look. Analyze your appearance objectively—the good points and the bad. This will help you to focus on how to reconcile your perception of yourself.

Put on an outfit that you feel really good in and ask yourself why. Then put on an outfit that you don't like and ask the same question. If you feel confident about this, then stand in front of the mirror in you bra and underpants and really look at your body. Don't be scared. Be objective as this is just between you and your mirror. Ask yourself these questions about the various parts of your body:

- What part is the thinnest?
- What part is the fullest?
- Are my shoulders and hips in line?
- Do I have a defined waist?
- Do I like my bust?
- Do I like my legs?

Then check what you find against the chart opposite and be honest, but positive, about yourself image.

Common concerns

You are not alone if you are not a standard shape and find shopping for clothes and dressing with confidence a cheerless experience. Here are some of the issues our models talked about during our photo shoots:

- I'm terrified of going up a size when I'm shopping for something new to wear.
- I find shopping very frustrating, I don't enjoy it at all.
- I've turned down invitations because I didn't feel confident that I could dress appropriately.
- Fashion magazines leave me uninspired.
- I've chosen vacation destinations that avoid having to go to a beach.
- I have a "fat" and a "thin" wardrobe to choose from.
- I try to avoid looking at myself in a mirror.

No doubt you share some of these concerns, but now is your chance to face them. Over the following pages, you will learn—with our models—how to improve your body image simply by wearing the right clothes.

RIGHT Emma has a very good shoulder line and chest and this neckline draws the eye there.

Emphasize the positive

The art of looking slimmer is not giving a name to your body shape, but learning how to make the most of your assets and disguising what you think are the least appealing attributes of your body.

How to analyze your appearance

What you would like to improve on	What you are happy with
Double chin	Lovely face
Short neck	Elegant neck
Short arms	Toned arms
Big bust	Cleavage
No waist definition	Defined waist
Short legs/long body or short body	Long legs/good body proportions
Rounded back	Good posture
Big stomach	Flat stomach
Big buttocks	Pert buttocks
Love handles	Curvaceous
Big hips	Feminine silhouette
Wide thighs/big knees	Shapely legs
No ankles	Fine ankles

The **soft, draping style** of this dress, together with the **fluid fabric,** flatters Nina's curvy body.

Your body shape

If you want to look slimmer and feel more confident when buying clothes, then it is crucial to consider how to dress all the individual parts of your body, rather than your entire body all at once.

Are you straight or curvy?

Although understanding your basic body shape is still important, working out whether your body is straight and angular or round and curvy will point you in the right direction for choosing clothing to make you look slimmer. It could also be that your upper body is straighter than your curvy lower half, or vice versa. The charts opposite will help you to decide what overall shape your body is.

Once you have determined which parts of you are straighter or curvier, you need to consider the actual construction of your clothes. Straighter bodies need straighter constructions; curvier bodies need softer and more shaped constructions.

If you found that you are a combination, then you might need straight constructions in soft fabrics. Perhaps a crisp cotton above the waist, with a softer fabric below, is the answer for you. Or try a shift dress in a soft jersey.

How to assess your upper body

	Straight	Curvy
Face	Square, rectangle, or oval	Oval or round
Shoulder line	Straight	Straight or curvy
Arms	Straight upper arms	Full upper arms
Bust	Small to average bust	Full bust
Back	Straight	Curved
Midriff/ rib cage	Straight	Curved
Waist	Not defined	Defined

How to assess your lower body

	Straight	Curvy
Stomach	Full	Full
Buttocks	Flattish	Curvy
Hips	Flattish	Curvy
Thighs	Slim	Full
Calves	Straight	Curvy
Ankles	Full	Shapely

Your scale

In order to achieve an overall look of balance and harmony, scale is something that you should consider not only when choosing clothes, but also accessories, such as jewelry and handbags.

What is scale?

Scale is determined by the actual size of your skeleton. When you carry extra weight, your external size will be larger, but your bone structure will remain constant. On a small-framed person in particular, 20 pounds will be much more noticeable than on a woman who has a large frame. No amount of weight gained or lost will change your bone structure.

SLIMMER STYLE TIP

Browse through your wardrobe and see if there are any pieces that you haven't worn. Take a look at the scale of the pattern, the buttons, or fabric weight. Do they break any of the rules on the opposite page? Now you know why this particular garment doesn't get a regular airing!

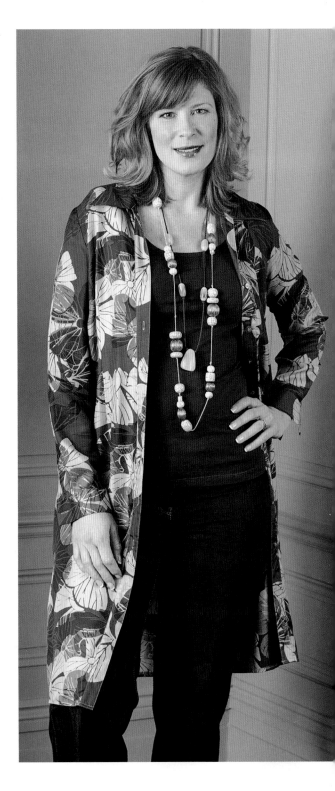

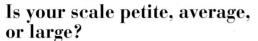

Is your scale petite, average, or large?

You may not have all the characteristics listed below, but see which category you most fit in to, as you may be a combination of two.

You are petite if:

- Your shoe size is under 6½
- You have slim ankles
- You have small wrists
- You have lean fingers
- You have a small face with fine features (small nose, lips, etc.).

You are average if:

- Your shoe size is between 6½ and 9
- Your wrist diameter is 6–7 inches
- Your glove size is small
- You have balanced facial features.

You are large if:

- Your shoe size is over 9
- Your wrist diameter is above 7 inches
- Your glove size is above medium
- You have a proportionally larger face.

How to dress for your scale

	Petite	Average	Large
Hairstyle	Keep neat	Balance with face size	Add volume (no close-cropped styles)
Pattern	Small	Average	Large
Fabric weight	Light to medium	Medium	Medium to heavy
Texture	Some, but not all over	Medium	Medium to heavy
Details (such as buttons, buckles, pockets)	Small	Medium	Medium to large
Accessories	Small or only one statement piece	Small in profusion or large with some constraint	Go for it!

LEFT The large-scale pattern of this fabric balances Amy's large bone structure.

Your proportions

Once you understand your proportions you can adjust the way you wear your clothes to give the illusion of a balanced body. The most successful outfits are those in which the waist appears to be in the center of the torso.

 WRONG
Nina is short-waisted and long-legged. When she tucks in, she looks unbalanced.

 RIGHT
Nina's best look is to wear her tops loose. This lengthens her torso, balancing well with her long legs.

High or low?

The effect of an unbalanced waistline on your appearance, and how your clothes fit and fall, is surprisingly important. If the waist appears high, the hips and buttocks will appear larger; if the waist is low, the top half of the body will appear proportionally longer, so you need to find a balance.

To check whether you are high- or low-waisted, you need to stand in front of a mirror and check where your waistline is.

You are high-waisted if:

- You generally don't tuck in
- You do not wear belts on your waistline
- You have a short midriff (little space between your bust and natural waistline)
- You often find pant legs are too short
- Your hips look high.

You are low-waisted if:

- Your tops feel too short
- Looking at yourself sideways, your buttocks appear low
- Pants fit you, but the legs are too long
- You do not like yourself in full skirts.

If you do not fit into either of these categories, then you are likely to have perfectly balanced proportions.

SLIMMER STYLE TIP

If you find that your pants come above your natural waistline, it might be that you are short in the rise, so look for low-rise pants. If the pants are tight and fall below your natural waistline, then you have a long rise, in which case high-rise pants will be best for you.

How to dress for your proportions

	High waist	Balanced	Low waist
Tops	Leave loose over waist or blouse over	You choose	Tuck in or belt
Waistband	None or lower	Leave as is	High or defined
Pants	Wider leg pants are good	You choose	You choose, but not too wide
Skirts	You choose	You choose	Minimum volume
Dresses	Low-waisted	You choose	Empire style is good
Shoes	Low heels or flats	You choose	Medium to high heels with open fronts

Some of this advice may vary, depending on your scale and height (see pages 16–17 and 20–21).

Your height and posture

Your height and, in particular, the way you hold yourself are part of your overall image. Both short and tall frames present their own challenges, but with careful choices you can still convey a slimmer you.

How tall are you?

You are short if you are under 5 feet 3 inches. You are average in height if you are 5 feet 3 inches–5 feet 6 inches. You are tall if you are over 5 feet 6 inches. The taller you are, the easier it will be to carry some extra weight. If you are shorter, the art of making yourself look taller will give the optical illusion of you being slimmer.

Posture

The way you stand can help you look slimmer and, in many ways, taller.

Signs of bad posture

- Do you slouch when seated, particularly at your work desk?
- Do you frequently stand on one leg, while resting the other?

LEFT Someone as tall as Michelle Obama (Deep; 5 feet 10 inches) carries her size both cleverly and elegantly.

RIGHT America Ferrera (Deep) is petite in height. By wearing a bright yellow coat over a black dress, she has combined colors to make herself look taller.

- When you bend down, do you bend your back rather than your knees?
- Are you seriously overweight? Extra weight will add strain to your muscles and joints.
- Do you have a full and heavy bust? This can sometimes lead to a rounded shoulder line as the shoulders and back take the strain of the weight of your bust. See pages 82–83 for correctly fitted bras.

Benefits of good posture

- A good posture will naturally create a straighter shoulder and a flatter stomach
- A straight back will not only help your abdominal muscles get a workout, but your clothes will hang from your shoulders rather than any fuller part of your body. So, shoulders back from now on! See pages 28–29 for shoulder styles.

Combining colors

Color is the key to success for many aspects of styling, and is especially useful when altering the perception of your height. So if you are short, by combining colors, you can make yourself look taller and, therefore, slimmer. See also pages 74–75.

SLIMMER STYLE TIP

If you feel your posture could do with some improvement, check out the Alexander Technique, yoga, or pilates.

Your bust, midriff, and waist

Women who carry extra weight are sometimes tempted to hide it all under ill-fitting or baggy clothes. However, it is possible to dress the upper part of your body to flatter and enhance it without resorting to the big cover-up.

Bust

Many women would love to change their bust, as the increased demand for breast enhancement and reduction over the past decade testifies. However, you can give the illusion of a smaller bust without resorting to such drastic measures. Simple adjustment to what you wear on, around, and over your bust will make you feel more confident with what nature has provided. The most important factor here is a correctly fitted bra (see pages 82–83 for how to ensure you wear the correct size and it is adjusted properly).

RIGHT A soft, draping neckline is always flattering on a full bust.

Getting it right

- Any details over the bust will draw attention to it, so, if you are full-breasted, do not wear tops with details such as pockets, embellishment, or logos, and ensure that your jewelry ends above or below the fullest part of your bust.
- A brooch worn to the side of the fullest part will draw the eye away.
- Those of you lucky enough to have a full bust may have a fantastic cleavage. This is an asset envied by many. Showing an appropriate amount of cleavage (how much you show depends on the occasion or environment you live or work in) can draw attention away from the fullest part of your chest and turn something that might give you concern into something that is an asset.

Midriff

This is the area between your bust and your waist. This is also, unfortunately for many, the place where extra fat seems to settle. You need to apply some thought as to how best to hide it if this is your concern.

Getting it right

- Tight, plain fabric pulled or stretched over this area will only make it more obvious.
- Fabric that has some detail either in its weave or texture will detract the eye to give a slimmer look.
- A belt or waistband worn tightly will only cause the midriff to roll over the top.
- Control-top panty hose or tights, shapewear panties, and too-small underpants can have the same effect. See pages 82–85 to select the correct underwear.
- Wearing patterns in this area will help disguise any fullness.

Waist

This is another area of the body that women have long-standing issues with. A defined waist is a wonderful asset, so show it off, if you have one, with belts and other details.

If you are short-waisted, use the advice given on pages 18–19 to give the illusion of lowering your waist slightly.

Getting it right

- Some women do not have a defined waist at all. Wearing absolutely straight or boxy clothes in crisp fabrics can add pounds to your look.
- Tops cut with some shaping at the waist will create the illusion of some definition around this area, thereby making you look slimmer.

BELOW A patterned top will disguise a full midriff successfully.

Tops and blouses

Having established your overall body shape and identified whether your upper body is straight or curvy, you can now start to select styles and details for tops that will flatter your shape, scale, and proportions.

LEFT The soft gathered top of this dress fits flatteringly on Amy's full bust.

Finding your style

The way the fabrics for your garments are cut and put together will either enhance or detract from your body lines. Recognizing minor details in, for example, collars or pockets, can give the illusion of you looking 1–2 pounds slimmer.

You should also consider the choice of fabric when choosing a top (see pages 42–43).

How to choose the right garment details for your upper body

Fronts	Suitable for
Concealed	Average to full bust
Double-breasted	Small to average bust; straight lines
Asymmetric	Small to average bust; straight lines
Wrap	Average to full bust
Ruched	Average to full (not very full)

Collar shapes	Suitable for
Straight	Straight lines
Shawl	Curvy lines
Jackie O	All
Waterfall	Large-scale straight or curvy

Seams	Suitable for
Straight	Small to average bust; straight lines
Princess	All

Pockets	Suitable for
Patched	Where you want to bring the eye
Sloping jetted	Jackets and coats
Concealed	Jackets and coats
Flap	Adding volume

SUITABLE TOP AND BLOUSE STYLES

For straight body shapes: Fitted shirt; ruched; wrap; bolero; vest; tank top; shaped blouse; asymmetric; polo shirt; shaped twin set.

For curvy body shapes: Cowl; gypsy; tied wrap; Empire line; kaftan; swing; shrug; scoop-neck T-shirt; classic twin set; ruffled blouse; loose shirt.

BELOW The crisp fabric and shape of Emma's shirt works with her straight upper body line.

Neckline styles

There are many different styles to choose from when it comes to neckline. Identifying the length of your neck will help you decide which of them are best for you. It will also help you to choose earrings and necklaces (see pages 92–93).

Finding your style

Take a look in a mirror to see whether you have a short or a long neck. Either can be flattered by a variety of styles, and if you fall somewhere in between, you can afford to try suitable styles from both groups to see which you like best.

You have a long neck if:

- You have a defined jaw line
- You feel uncomfortable in a low neckline
- You feel physically comfortable wearing a turtleneck sweater

If you have a long neck and you want to wear an open neckline, you will need to fill the area with jewelry or a scarf. You also have the choice of wearing a camisole underneath an open neckline.

When it comes to wearing jewelry, opt for a multiple of different-length necklaces to fill any open area between your chin and neckline. They can vary in style and color. A choker-style necklace will also flatter when worn with a low-cut evening dress, as long as your neck is not too wide. Choose long dangling earrings or large hoops.

LEFT A turtleneck sweater is elegant on a long neck.

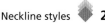

RIGHT Lisa's scoop-neck top is flattering, and allows for some flesh to be on show.

You have a short neck if:

- You have a double chin
- Your jowls blend into your neck
- You are uncomfortable wearing anything around your neck.

If you have a short neck, and you want to wear a higher neckline, it must be open at the front to give the illusion of a slimmer, longer neck. Keep your neck uncluttered with jewelry or scarves.

When it comes to jewelry, choose necklaces that sit just below the collarbone. They can be multi-stranded or single with a statement decoration. A long necklace can work if you are full-busted, but keep it away from the fullest part of your bust. Keep earrings close to your face, and avoid any that dangle too close to your shoulders.

SUITABLE NECKLINE STYLES

For long necks: Mandarin; turtleneck; stand-up collar; shirt collar up; ruffle; flounce.

For short necks: Shirt collar down; flounce; cowl; sweetheart; square; boatneck; Bardot; jeweled; scoop-neck; V-neck.

Shoulder styles

When clothes hang properly from the shoulders, they fall more elegantly, giving a slimmer look to your upper body. However, this does not mean that you always need to wear a stiff formal shoulder line, for there are plenty of styles to choose from.

Finding your style

There are plenty of clothing styles to choose from when it comes to shoulders. First, you must determine what type of shoulders you have. Take a look in the mirror to find out.

You have straight shoulders if:
Your shoulders are at a right angle to your neck, and flat.
If you have straight shoulders, aim to keep the shoulder line straight and avoid bulky details.

You have rounded shoulders if:
Your shoulders are soft and curvy.
Softer seaming is ideal for you if you have a rounded shoulder line. It is best to avoid a firm shoulder line.

You have sloping shoulders if:
Your shoulders slant down from the neck.
You will always benefit from a little padding if you have sloping shoulders. This helps to balance the silhouette, making you appear slimmer.

TO PAD OR NOT TO PAD?

Shoulder pads, even when not in fashion, could be your best friends. They come in different sizes, weights, and shapes—we are not talking '80s power dressing! Finding the right ones for you may require a trip to a sewing notions department, wearing a soft sweater, and trying them on to see the effect.

- Shoulder pads are great to give the illusion of balance if you have narrow or sloping shoulders.

- Straight body shapes may benefit from wearing pads in soft-fabric garments. For curvy bodies, shoulder pads will give a more formal and constructed look to their softer-line garments.

- Make sure that once you have found the right shoulder pads for you, you get them in all available colors (usually black, white, and neutral) and that they fit unobstructively under your clothes.

You have narrow shoulders if:

Your shoulders are noticeably smaller than your hips.

Details on the edge of the shoulders will give you more width if you have narrow shoulders. Avoid wearing cutout sleeves.

You have wide shoulders if:

Your shoulders are noticeably wider than your hips.

Raglan and cutout shoulder lines are great if you have wide shoulders. You should avoid dropped shoulders and details on the edge of the shoulder, such as puff sleeves or fringes.

SUITABLE SHOULDER STYLES

For straight shoulders: Strapless; off the shoulder; halter top; asymmetric; inserted; raglan.

For rounded shoulders: Strapless; off the shoulder; inserted; gathered; dropped; dolman.

For sloping shoulders: Strapless; inserted (with pads); gathered; dolman (with pads).

For narrow shoulders: Strapless, off the shoulder; inserted; gathered; dropped.

For wide shoulders: Strapless, off the shoulder; halter top; asymmetric; raglan.

LEFT Emma has a straight shoulder line. The strap details of this dress complement her perfectly.

An interesting **detail on the sleeve** can help to **detract the eye** from an unflattering area.

Arm and sleeve styles

Your arms may well be one of your best assets. With a few basic tricks, you can learn how to dress them up, whatever the occasion or the weather, to give the illusion of slender and even longer arms.

Finding your style

You can usually tell from the garments that you buy whether or not your arms are long or short in proportion to the rest of your upper body. Both can be flattered by wearing a variety of styles. If you fall somewhere in between, try suitable styles from both groups to see which you like best.

You have short arms if:

Most purchased garments in your size are too long in the sleeve.

Wherever possible you will need to shorten the sleeve (this must be done for jackets and coats). Alternatively, you can push them up toward the elbow, as long as they don't bulk up too much.

You have long arms if:

Most purchased garments in your size reveal a gap between your wrist and your hand.

You can compensate for this gap by filling it with a large watch or bracelets.

Getting it right

The upper arms are not always the most attractive part of the arm. Wearing the right sleeve and length can make the arms look slimmer.

- Do not hesitate to wear sleeveless tops if your upper arms are firm and toned. Make sure, though, that you exfoliate regularly and use good body lotion to ensure a smooth silky skin.
- If your upper arms are wide, avoid at all costs any type of short sleeves. If you want the illusion of a short sleeve, a split sleeve or kimono style, where the hemline is fluid, will be more flattering.
- Any sleeve finishing on the forearms is flattering, except if you have very long arms.

SUITABLE ARM AND SLEEVE STYLES

For short to average arms: Sleeveless; cap; elbow; three-quarter length; bracelet; wrist length; short flared; cuffed; petal; split.

For average to long arms: Short; elbow; three-quarter length; bracelet; wrist length; short flared; cuffed; petal; split; puffed short and long; long flared; ruffled; batwing; bell.

Your hips, buttocks, and legs

Tight clothes always add weight, so getting the correct fit over the lower half of your body will help to give the appearance of a slimmer you. Simply changing the shape of your skirt or pants will help to disguise that extra weight.

Hips

Look at your hips straight on in a mirror. Do they run almost straight from your waist to your thighs, or do they curve out, giving you a feminine shape?

Getting it right

- If you want to make your hips look smaller, do not clutter the outer edges with pockets and embellishments.
- Ensure that your tops, shirts, and jackets finish above or below the widest point on your hips. A jacket that finishes above the widest point will draw attention away from your hips.
- Do not fall into the trap of always wearing long, baggy tops.
- If you have flat hips, you may want to add interest to the sides, such as pockets or any form of decoration, to give you a more feminine look; this will also help to balance a full bust. Ending any top here will also make the hips appear wider.

Buttocks

Now look at your buttocks sideways in a mirror. Is there a straightish line from your waist to the top of your thighs? Or do your buttocks curve out and around? Nothing looks worse than a tight fit around the buttocks in both skirts and pants, especially with a full visible panty line (VPL).

Getting it right

- Rounded, curvy buttocks need skirts and pants that are either shaped with darts or some easing of the waist to accommodate the curves.
- It is more flattering and slimming if the fabric hangs from the fullest part of your buttocks rather than curving around and under.
- Avoid details in the buttock area if rounded.
- Flattish buttocks can be embellished with pockets and other details.

Legs

Your legs, ankles, and feet are the most hard-working parts of your body and sometimes they are neglected. Often, the major challenge women have is the fullness of their thighs. For some women, their thighs are disproportionately larger than their hips, and this causes many frustrating hours spent in the stores looking for clothes that not only fit, but make them look slimmer. The choice will then come down to probably deciding to wear a skirt or dress, or being very selective when choosing fabric for pants.

Getting it right

- Whether you are wearing a skirt or pants, the golden rule is that they must finish at a narrow point of your leg.
- Minimize the volume of the fabrics of your skirts and pants if you have shorter legs.
- If you have thick ankles, avoid ankle straps on shoes at all costs as these "cut" into the leg and draw the eye.
- If you must have straps, match the color to your panty hose or tights so it doesn't show, and ensure that your panty hose are the same color as your hemline to elongate the leg (see page 84).
- Create the illusion of longer legs with a split in your skirt, whether front, back, or side.

LEFT Christie's sweater emphasizes her curves, finishing just above the widest point on her buttocks. Her soft, bias-cut skirt hangs straight for a slimmer look.

Skirts and pants

Armed with an honest approach to your general lower body shape, you can now start to select styles and details for skirts and pants that will enhance your assets and create a sleeker look.

Finding your style

When choosing skirts and pants, don't forget to consider the details—they can make all the difference to the success of your new style. See also pages 42–43 for careful choice of fabrics and patterns.

SUITABLE SKIRT AND PANT STYLES

For straight body shapes: Pencil skirt; crossover skirt; tulip skirt; paneled skirt; narrow pleats; bootleg pants; jeans; crease-fronted pants; narrow leg; cropped pants.

For curvy body shapes: Bias cut; wrap; flip; asymmetric; circular; culottes; harem; full leg; straight; drawstring pants; palazzo.

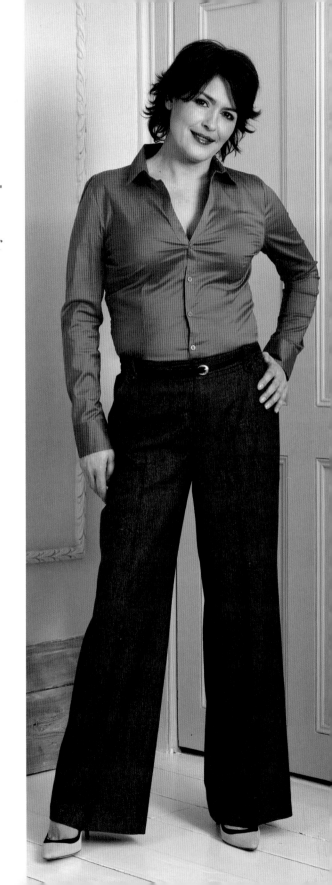

RIGHT Emma wears flat-fronted pants. The crease gives a crisp line to her shape.

How to choose the right garment details for your lower body

Waistbands	Suitable for
No waistband	Full waist; high-waisted
High waistband	Defined waist; low-waisted
Hipster	Full and/ or high-waisted
Hipster banded	Full and/ or high-waisted
Elasticated	Comfort in soft fabrics for all
Drawstring	Comfort in soft fabrics for all
Martingale	All

SLIMMER STYLE TIP

If you feel your legs are a little short, narrow leg pants and pencil skirts will make you appear taller and, therefore, slimmer.

Shaping	Suitable for
Flat-fronted	All
Darts	Curvy lines
Tucks	Curvy lines
Structured peplum on jackets	Flat or pert buttocks
Soft peplum on jackets	Curvy buttocks

Pleats	Suitable for
Narrow	Straight lines
Box	Straight lines
Stitched-down	Straight lines
Gathers	Curvy lines, but not too full

Zippers	Suitable for
Concealed	All
Placket	Flat stomach
Exposed	Flat stomach

Hemlines	Suitable for
Asymmetric	Shapely legs
Paneled	All
Flounce	Long legs

Dresses and evening wear

In the past decade, dresses have become a must-have in everyone's wardrobe. Avoid the temptations and frustrations of ill-fitting, high-fashion trends and discover a dress style for you that is feminine and flattering.

Finding your style

Dresses are a combination of all the previous pages in this chapter, and, therefore, when you find the right style or styles of dress for you, make them a staple of your wardrobe. Deciding on a style of dress that really works for you will save a lot of time and effort, because you will discover that the same style can work for many different occasions, from a formal event to the beach. A dress is also a very good alternative to a suit for work, as you can wear it alone, or with a contrasting or complementary jacket or even a cardigan or wrap. Finally, you can dress up a simple dress for the evening, whatever the style, by adding a stunning piece of jewelry, fancy pany hose, and different shoes.

Straight body shapes

A shift dress in wool gabardine is perfect for a woman with a straighter body shape and can be worn long or short, and with or without sleeves, depending on preference and occasion. You can also wear an Empire-style dress, which has a high-waist emphasis just below the bust. Dresses with high collars (shirt dresses) and turtlenecks work well, as do those with pleated or paneled skirts. If you opt for a belted dress, make sure your waist is neither high nor low, as you could end up making your body look unbalanced. Sleeves should finish at a narrow point on your arm: often elbow, three-quarter, or wrist length.

Curved body shapes

The ideal dresses for curved bodies are those made from soft fabric. A wrap dress is a good option and will come in different weights, depending on the season. Other styles that suit you include dresses with bias-cut skirts and A-line dresses, which work well for almost any height and proportions. If you find that you are different sizes top and bottom, you could opt for separates, which also offer great scope for coordinating colors. As for straight bodies, sleeves should finish at a narrow point on your arm, and keep sleeve details simple. Avoid any styles that have pockets.

SUITABLE DRESS STYLES

For straight body shapes: Shift; low-waisted; coat dress; spaghetti strap shift; semifitted princess line; tulip; fishtail; tuxedo.

For curvy body shapes: Shirt-dress shape with soft belt (no pockets); A-line; wrap; sack dress; princess line; bias cut; tea dress; ball gown.

This **softly draped dress** enhances Laura's curves. It emphasizes her small waist and **flows gently** over her fuller hips.

Veronique's coat combines **soft lines and wool fabric**. The **jetted pockets** are perfect for a slimmer look.

Jackets and coats

We cannot emphasize enough the importance of the type of fabrics you choose for your jackets and coats. Buying the right cut of jacket or coat for your body shape is also crucial to achieving a slim and flattering body line.

Finding your style

Your scale, proportions, and height are all factors that you need to consider (see pages 16–21), along with the type and thickness of fabric. Women with small frames must be careful not to bulk up with heavy fabrics and too many layers.

Often, women may buy a jacket in a size to accommodate a full bust or broad back, which will result in too much fabric around the shoulders and overlong sleeves.

Straight body shapes

Many women with a straight body line have little waist definition, so look for jackets and coats that give the illusion of a waist, which will make you appear slimmer.

Curvy body shapes

Curvy women who need formal work wear will be better advised to wear a long, deconstructed coat or cardigan in a knit or soft wool, rather than a short, fitted jacket in a heavy fabric, which will restrict their movements and make them look bulkier. Unlined jackets and coats will be less bulky and more comfortable for a slimmer look.

Practicalities

Often a coat will be an investment that you make every other year, or every few years. Making sure that you buy the right one for you and your lifestyle requires some consideration. If you wear a coat only occasionally, then maybe you should consider a raincoat, which may have a warm-lining option. If you are in and out of the car, then choosing a heavy-weight jacket or three-quarter-length coat might be best for you. If you walk a lot in cold weather, then a long-length one will be more appropriate.

SUITABLE JACKET AND COAT STYLES

For straight body shapes: Single- or double-breasted jackets and coats; rever jacket; edge-to-edge cardigan; boyfriend jacket; zipper jacket; long heavy-knit cardigan.

For curvy body shapes: Deconstructed jacket; waterfall jacket; belted cardigan; shawl-collar jacket; wrap jacket; long, wrap coat; swing coat.

The right fit

Tight-fitting garments and loose, baggy clothing can both add weight to your look. Making sure your clothes fit (and this does not mean that they are fitted) will ensure you achieve a slimmer look, whatever your size.

The golden rules

Here are some basic rules which, when observed, will ensure that you look well dressed and your clothes were made for you.

- All clothes manufacturers' sizes will vary, so do not insist on one size if a larger (or smaller) size fits better.
- American and European standard sizes vary greatly, so make sure you try on clothes before you buy them.
- Zippers should lie flat and, if covered, remain so.
- Seams should lie straight on the garment when worn and should not pull.
- Pockets should not gape.

Tops and blouses

- Shoulder seams should be on the edge of the shoulder or just over.
- Long sleeves should finish at the wrist bone.
- Sleeves should be wide enough to permit comfortable movement.
- Buttons should remain closed and not pull at the bust.

LEFT Laura demonstrates that looking good is about showing her figure to her best advantage.

Jackets

- Collars should sit flat around the neck and across the shoulders and not gape.
- Jackets should lie flat across the bust and not pucker (if this happens, it means the fabric is too stiff for your body shape).
- There should be no pulling across the back.
- The bottom of the jacket should not finish at the widest point of your hips or buttocks.

Skirts

- Skirts should hang straight from the buttocks and not curve under.
- Waistlines should be loose enough to enable you to turn the skirt around easily (say, for zipping up).
- Pleats should lie flat.
- Hemlines should hang straight and end at a narrow point on your legs.

Pants

- The legs should hang straight from the hips and not curve under the buttocks, unless designed to do so.
- The waistband should be big enough so that your midriff does not show.
- Pant legs should not cling to fuller thighs.

Fabrics and patterns

When shopping for clothes, most women concentrate on the size of a garment rather than on the fabric it is made of, or its pattern if it has one. If you choose these correctly, it is often possible to drop a size to achieve a slimmer look.

Identifying fabrics

Fabrics are often a mix of up to four different yarns—some natural, some man-made. Combination fabrics are designed for comfort and easy care.

Weight, texture, fluidity

You will find cottons, wools, silks, and linens of various weights, textures, and fluidity, depending on the mix of yarns, and you need to bear in mind the following:

- The heavier the fabric, the more bulk it will add to the silhouette.
- Texture can add volume.
- Crisper fabrics work best on straight bodies.
- Curves are better dressed in soft, fluid fabric.

Lycra is your best friend

Manufacturers have found the joys of Lycra. Not only does it give ease in a fabric, but in its heavier form it can also help to keep under control those extra pounds.

To shine or not to shine?

Shiny fabric in all its forms will draw attention to where it is positioned.

The cut of it

The way in which the fabric is cut also influences the way it falls and its fluidity. For example, linen cut on the straight of the grain will hang straight and crisply, while if it is cut across the grain (on the bias), it will flow and drape in a softer manner. Bias cutting is particularly good across any curves and fullness of the body.

LEFT Amy looks stunning in this swirl-patterned jersey dress.

Thinking about pattern

Pattern is a fun way to introduce color and follow the trends. It will also help to detract or draw the attention, depending on where the pattern is. Think carefully about your scale (see pages 16–17) and that of the pattern to ensure they work in harmony.

How to choose the right pattern for your body shape

	Straight	Curvy
Stripes	All	Blended thin, vertical
Geometrics	All	Soft edges
Plaids and tartans	All	Not really suitable
Paisley/ swirls	Not suitable	All
Florals	Abstract florals only	All
Polka dots/ animal print	All	All
Water-color/ tie-dye	Not suitable	All

RIGHT Many women are wary of wearing stripes, but when worn correctly, they can look stunning. Stripes are perfect for Emma's straight lines.

slimmer colors

The right colors for you

Now that you understand what to look for when choosing your clothes in terms of shape and style, you need to consider the colors you wear. Through clever combinations, the right colors can give the impression of a slimmer you.

The theory

colour me beautiful is the authority on color analysis, based on the Munsell theory that identifies three characteristics of color: hue, value, and chroma. Each of these characteristics appears in every single color. Most colors will have one dominant characteristic, and it is this that we will use to describe your coloring in this book.

Hue, or undertone, defines whether a color is warm (yellow-based) or cool (blue-based).

Value, or depth, is how light or how dark a color is; this is sometimes described on a scale, devised by Munsell, from 0 to 10, with 0 being black and 10 being white.

Chroma, or clarity, indicates how clear and bright a color is, or how soft and muted it is. Clear and bright colors reflect the light and soft, muted colors seem to absorb light.

We will show you the best ways to combine colors to help you give the illusion of shedding those pounds. Careful consideration of how you put colors together will not only help to make you look slimmer, but will also help you create a workable wardrobe of fewer clothes, but more wearable combinations.

Wearing color

There are thousands of shades of colors available and some will make you look radiant, while others will make you look unhealthy and tired. Wearing the right color near your face—and wearing the right shades of make-up—will make you look younger, healthier, and even slimmer. When you have identified your own coloring type (see pages 48–49), you will be able to choose the right colors for you from the color groups on the following pages.

SLIMMER STYLE TIP
Black does not necessarily make you look slimmer. It will only work if it is a color that is in your palette. There are many other colors that can make you look slimmer—navy, brown, pine, purple, and charcoal, to name just a few.

RIGHT Kelly Clarkson (Soft) is wearing a colorful dress that perfectly suits her soft coloring.
FAR RIGHT Jennifer Hudson (Deep) wears a shiny fabric that shows off her full bust.

Identify your coloring

At **colour me beautiful,** we work with the theory that you need to wear colors that are in harmony and balance with your natural coloring. We describe colors using these terms: light, deep, warm, cool, clear, and soft.

Finding your dominant coloring

Look carefully at yourself and note down:

- The color of your hair as it is today, whether natural or tinted.
- The color of your eyes—if you are not sure, ask a friend.
- The tone of your skin: pale, medium or dark.

Now compare your checklist to the descriptions opposite to identify which dominant coloring most resembles yours and how to wear your colors.

The colors you'll wear need to be in harmony and balance with your own physical looks. Remember that if you change your hair color, your dominant coloring may change, too.

If you feel you are a little of every description, you may well be a Soft.

Light

Hair: Naturally blonde
Eyes: Light blue, green, or pale brown
Skin: Pale

How to wear your colors

Your overall look is light and delicate, and although you might avoid light colors, you should wear them near your face to avoid unwanted shadows.

Deep

Hair: Dark brown or black
Eyes: Dark brown
Skin: Pale to dark skin

How to wear your colors

Yes, you will look great in black, but don't overdo it, and learn to use other colors to give the impression of confidence and well-being.

Warm

Hair: Red or auburn
Eyes: Green, blue, or brown
Skin: Pale skin, with freckles

How to wear your colors

Your best colors will always be those with a yellow or warm undertone. If you wear navies and grays, warm them up with other colors from your palette.

Clear

Hair: Dark brown or black
Eyes: Bright green, blue, or topaz
Skin: Pale to dark

How to wear your colors

The secret to wearing your colors with the most effect is to contrast the depth—light against dark. If wearing just one color, make it a bright one.

Cool

Hair: Ash-colored or gray
Eyes: Blue-grey
Skin: Medium-tone, rosy

How to wear your colors

Do not be afraid to use some brighter colors with your dark, neutral colors. Brown should not feature in your wardrobe, but try grays, navies, and greens.

Soft

Hair: Medium-tone, highlighted mousy hair
Eyes: Soft-blended blue, green-hazel tones
Skin: Medium

How to wear your colors

Wearing colors from the same family of color (such as all blues, or all browns) will give you a tone-on-tone effect for an elegant and slimming look.

Beautiful blues

Blue is a safe color that most people enjoy wearing. It is also known to have healing and calming effects on the wearer.

	Light	Deep	Warm	Cool	Clear	Soft
1 Icy blue	✓			✓	✓	
2 Eau de nil						✓
3 Powder blue	✓			✓		
4 Sky blue	✓			✓	✓	✓
5 Bluebell	✓					✓
6 Light periwinkle	✓		✓			✓
7 Periwinkle		✓	✓			✓
8 Cornflower blue	✓	✓		✓	✓	
9 Sapphire				✓		✓
10 True blue		✓		✓	✓	
11 Lapis		✓	✓		✓	
12 Royal blue		✓		✓	✓	

The **soft, blended blue tones** of Veronique's kaftan complement her **cool coloring**.

Perfect purples

The berry colors make a rich and glorious addition to any wardrobe, and offer a great alternative to black.

	Light	Deep	Warm	Cool	Clear	Soft
1 Fuchsia				✓		
2 Cassis				✓		
3 Plum		✓		✓		
4 Amethyst						✓
5 Soft violet	✓					✓
6 Lavender	✓			✓		✓
7 Violet	✓			✓		
8 Bright periwinkle				✓	✓	
9 Purple	✓		✓		✓	✓
10 Royal purple		✓				
11 Eggplant		✓				
12 Damson		✓				✓

The **blended tones** of Sarah's cardigan and top balance well with her **soft coloring**.

Red gives you **confidence and energy**. Here it creates a vibrant look with Christie's **deep coloring**.

Dynamic reds

Reds are wonderfully energizing colors—a red raincoat is a great addition to any wardrobe to cheer up a dull day.

	Light	Deep	Warm	Cool	Clear	Soft
1 Geranium	✓					✓
2 True red		✓			✓	
3 Orange-red			✓			
4 Bittersweet		✓	✓			
5 Tomato		✓	✓			
6 Scarlet		✓			✓	
7 Watermelon	✓		✓		✓	
8 Raspberry		✓		✓		
9 Ruby					✓	
10 Blue-red				✓		
11 Claret						✓
12 Burgundy		✓				✓

Pretty pinks

Every woman needs feminine pinks, but getting the right shade is essential if you are going to achieve a mature look.

	Light	Deep	Warm	Cool	Clear	Soft
1 Light apricot	✓		✓		✓	
2 Apricot			✓			
3 Clear salmon			✓		✓	
4 Salmon pink		✓	✓			✓
5 Coral pink			✓			✓
6 Blush pink	✓	✓				✓
7 Baby pink				✓		
8 Candy				✓	✓	
9 Orchid				✓		✓
10 Hot pink				✓		
11 Rose		✓		✓		✓
12 Cyclamen				✓	✓	

This fun combination of **warm and cool pinks** in Mel's outfit works beautifully with her **light coloring**.

Lime and terra cotta work together to give Amy a golden glow to her **warm coloring**.

Citrus colors

These are sunshine colors; if you do not have them in your palette, add some lighter greens to achieve the same effect.

	Light	Deep	Warm	Cool	Clear	Soft
1 Primrose	✓		✓			
2 Light gold	✓		✓			
3 Mustard		✓	✓			
4 Amber			✓			
5 Tangerine			✓			
6 Terra cotta			✓			
7 Icy green	✓			✓		
8 Light moss			✓			✓
9 Lime		✓	✓			
10 Apple green	✓				✓	
11 Fern		✓			✓	
12 Verbena						✓

The striking colors of these **aquas and turquoises** make a stunning combination for Laura's **clear coloring**.

Sea greens

Warm greens have a yellow undertone, while cool greens tend to be more blue. These tropical shades lift any neutrals.

	Light	Deep	Warm	Cool	Clear	Soft
1 Mint	✓				✓	✓
2 Sea green	✓			✓		
3 Peppermint				✓		
4 Jade	✓					✓
5 Peacock	✓					
6 Emerald turquoise		✓	✓		✓	✓
7 Turquoise		✓	✓			✓
8 Light teal	✓			✓	✓	
9 Light aqua	✓			✓	✓	
10 Aqua		✓	✓		✓	
11 Chinese blue		✓			✓	
12 Dark teal	✓					✓

Neutrals: Light

As a Light, you should wear the lighter shades near your face. None of your neutrals are particularly dark. If you have to wear black, keep it away from your face, and team it with a light neutral or a light shade from your color palette.

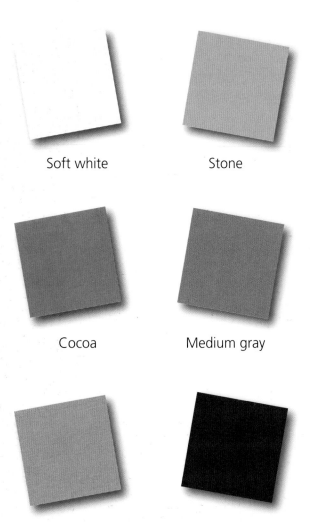

Soft white

Stone

Cocoa

Medium gray

Sage

Light navy

Your neutrals

Your neutrals are all very elegant and sophisticated shades. You have the choice of wearing them tone-on-tone—for example, cocoa with stone—or contrasting them with some of the brighter colors in your palette. The challenge for you is dressing appropriately in winter, as you are limited in the number of darker colors in your palette. Navy is your obvious choice as an alternative to black, but medium gray and cocoa are also superb alternatives. The secret to wearing any color combination is always to have the right color as close to your face as possible. Remember that you can always add color to your neutrals with accessories, whether beads, necklaces, or scarves. Think about using brighter colors for shoes and purses as well.

Some color combinations to try:

- Soft white + Cornflower blue or Light periwinkle
- Stone + Geranium or Watermelon
- Cocoa + Light teal or Sea green
- Medium gray + Light apricot or Blush pink
- Sage + Soft violet or Lavender
- Light navy + Primrose or Icy green

Mel is wearing a beautiful **stone evening top,** which is stunning against her **light coloring.**

Christie's cardigan in **contrasting teal** over her dark brown top **draws the attention away from her bust.**

Neutrals: Deep

As a Deep, remember to keep dark colors near your face. If you want to wear a light color, combine it with a darker neutral or a bright color from your palette. When wearing lighter neutrals, wear a bright color and avoid white.

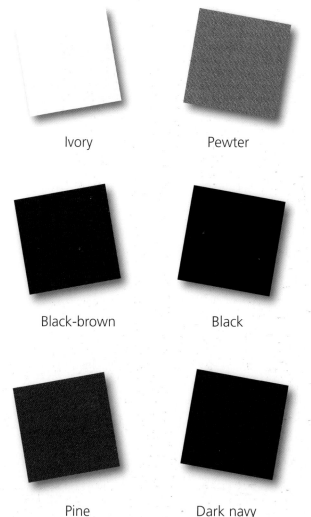

Ivory

Pewter

Black-brown

Black

Pine

Dark navy

Your neutrals

You have a broad selection of neutrals that you can wear all year round, from ivory to black. The secret is always to keep the darker shades near your face. Your strong features allow you to wear two dark colors together, or a light and dark combination; you should avoid pale colors on their own. In warmer weather, use ivory and pewter as the basis for your wardrobe, mixing with all the brighter shades from your palette. Remember to assess which parts of your body you want to draw attention to and wear the brightest or lightest color there. Wear the darkest colors where you want the least attention. Also remember when wearing darker colors that you need to adjust your makeup colors to suit (see page 99).

Some color combinations to try:

- Ivory + Plum or Eggplant
- Pewter + True red or Burgundy
- Black-brown + Rose or Salmon pink
- Black + Mustard or Fern
- Pine + Emerald turquoise or Aqua
- Dark navy + True blue or Lapis

Neutrals: Warm

As a Warm, the colors you wear near your face need to have a warm (or yellow) undertone. Black is not in your palette, but charcoal will work for you, as long as you warm it up with yellows, corals, and warm reds.

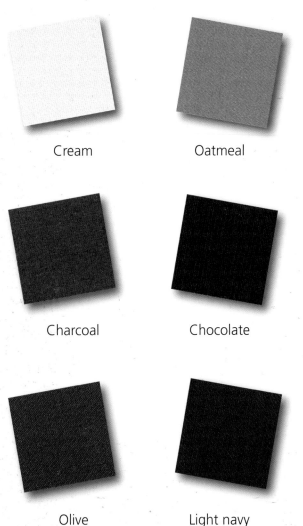

Cream

Oatmeal

Charcoal

Chocolate

Olive

Light navy

Your neutrals

As someone with warm coloring, you have a wonderful selection of shades that will complement the warm tones of your hair, skin, and eye color. All are great substitutes for black and will avoid you having to wear overpowering makeup to balance your look. In the warmer months, you will be able to have cream and oatmeal as the core neutrals in your wardrobe, not forgetting that light navy may be worn all year around. You can also wear your neutrals together for an interesting look: oatmeal and light navy are both great. Remember you may also wear gold or warm-colored accessories to warm up your light navy and charcoal gray. Brown and tan shoes, boots, and purses are also fun to have with these colors.

Some color combinations to try:

- Cream + Purple or Coral pink
- Oatmeal + Turquoise or Aqua
- Charcoal + Apricot or Salmon pink
- Chocolate + Light periwinkle or Periwinkle
- Olive + Amber or Lime
- Light navy + Orange red or Tomato

Amy has **combined two of her neutrals, olive and chocolate**, with lime to give an interesting look to a formal outfit.

Adding **contrasting pearls and sparkles** to this top gives Veronique the **clarity** that she needs.

Neutrals: Cool

Cool shades have a blue undertone to them. When wearing your neutrals, be confident and add some contrasting colors to them. If you need to wear black, use your pinks to give yourself a healthy glow.

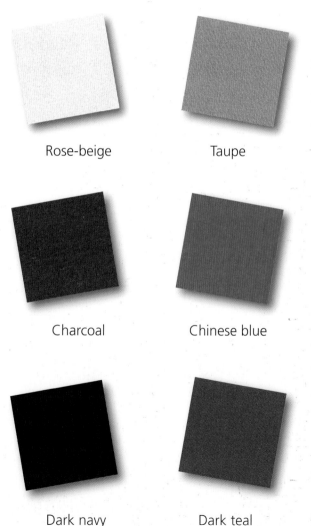

Rose-beige

Taupe

Charcoal

Chinese blue

Dark navy

Dark teal

Your neutrals

Your cool coloring gives you the opportunity of wearing some striking neutrals, especially when worn in contrast with other shades from your palette. It is possible that you have become cool as the years have passed, so do try experimenting with shades that you may never have been tempted to wear before. Your neutrals are a great place to start. Black is in your palette, but is always best worn with a light shade near the face. Alternatively, you can lift it with some bright and sparkling jewelry. If your hair has changed color and you wear glasses, remember the frames of your glasses should be in either one of your neutral shades or a color from your palette. As your coloring has changed, so should your makeup shades (see page 101) to coordinate with the cool undertone of your clothes.

Some color combinations to try:

- Rose-beige + Raspberry or Blue-red
- Taupe + Fuchsia or Bright periwinkle
- Charcoal + Baby pink or Cyclamen
- Chinese blue + Sea green or Light aqua
- Dark navy + Icy blue or Sapphire
- Dark teal + Icy green or Light teal

Neutrals: Clear

Clear colors are bright and should be worn as a contrast. If you are not comfortable wearing bright colors, you can achieve a slimmer look by combining neutrals with brightly colored accessories.

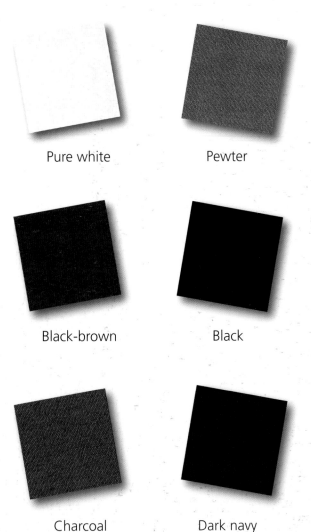

Pure white

Pewter

Black-brown

Black

Charcoal

Dark navy

Your neutrals

You have some really strong colors for your neutrals, but you must avoid wearing the darker shades on their own or in any combination together. Black is a great color for you, and you can have fun adding brighter shades or striking accessories in colors that you feel comfortable with. Your neutral colors are also suitable for your accessories. An investment black or navy bag will have great longevity in anyone's wardrobe, and a colorful scarf will give you a brighter color combination that works for you. When it comes to makeup, try either strong eye makeup colors or a stronger lipstick, but not both together. Bring contrast to your neutrals with sparkling necklaces, brooches, earrings, and brightly colored frames for glasses.

Some color combinations to try:

- Pure white + Royal blue or True blue
- Pewter + Bright periwinkle or Purple
- Black-brown + Apple green or Fern
- Black + Clear salmon or Candy
- Charcoal + Ruby or Scarlet
- Dark navy + Mint or Chinese blue

The strong **contrast of the large-scale white polka dots on black** are a great look on Laura.

Nina's dress is knitted, so the **texture of the fabric** also helps to soften the color as well as **complement her curvy figure**.

Neutrals: Soft

All your colors have a soft or muted appearance. A small amount of contrast may be used, but high contrast combining dark and light colors together will overpower you. A key to your look is to mix and match your neutrals.

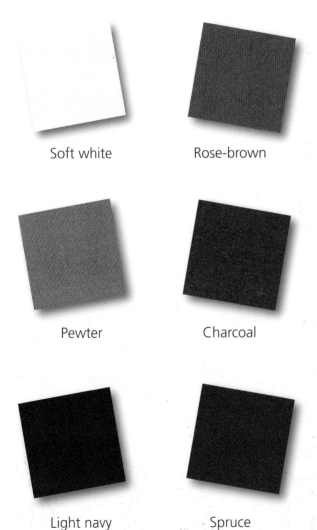

Soft white

Rose-brown

Pewter

Charcoal

Light navy

Spruce

Your neutrals

Your look is one where you combine your neutrals in soft contrast or blended tones. You can achieve a really elegant and slimming look by mixing your neutrals together, so think about two or three of them as core pieces for your wardrobe. When it comes to adding color, try to keep the depth of color the same and avoid high contrast. Accessories, such as shoes and purses, should be in colors that blend with your neutrals and not in shades that add high contrast. When thinking about adding jewellery or glasses to an outfit, toning shades will always be more flattering, as will matte surfaces rather than very shiny ones. The addition of a soft, tonal scarf will help to make black more acceptable, as will fabric that has a soft pile surface or a matte finish.

Some color combinations to try:

- Soft white + Light moss or Verbena
- Rose-brown + Coral pink or Orchid
- Pewter + Amethyst or Damson
- Charcoal + Claret or Burgundy
- Light navy + Bluebell or Periwinkle
- Spruce + Jade or Dark teal

Combining colors

By combining colors, you can make yourself look both taller and slimmer. Where and how you wear your darker colors is essential to creating a look that gives the illusion of a slimmer you.

Getting it right

In addition to colors, you need to consider your scale (see pages 16–17), your proportions (pages 18–19), and, of course, your height (pages 20–21). Here are a few tips for getting it right:

- Make sure your choice of color actually works for your lifestyle. Sometimes you may need to darken a shade if you have an occupation for which a more formal dress code is required; this is especially important if your coloring is light.
- One color from head to toe always gives the illusion of height.
- Use neutral or dark colors to minimize any large feature.
- For those of you with narrow shoulders or fuller stomach or hips, brighter colors worn near the face will draw attention away from these areas.
- Darker skirts and pants help to minimize larger hips and thighs.
- Use brightly colored accessories with neutrals.
- Unless you have long legs, always try to team the hosiery with the hemline color.

SLIMMER STYLE TIP FOR PETITES
If wearing a short skirt and you want to give yourself more height, make sure your hosiery tones or matches with the color of the skirt. The maximum number of colors you should put together is two.

Same shade or color
Wearing one color from head to toe will always give the illusion of height. This is key for petites, those under 5 feet 3 inches (1.6 m).

Paler top

This combination works for all, unless you have a very full bust. It helps to give the illusion of wider shoulders, which will balance fuller hips.

Darker top

This combination is particularly good for those with a very full bust, or those with very wide or heavy shoulders, or with fuller arms.

Three-color combination

To wear a three-color combination you need to be tall, over 5 feet 6 inches. If you are shorter, replace the short skirt with a long skirt.

Paler bottom

This combination is great if you have flat hips and buttocks. It is a good idea to add details or embellishments with this combination.

Wardrobe management

To create a hard-working wardrobe, you will need to focus on your neutrals as the most important pieces. These will work well with any other colors from your palette and make it easy to put together coordinated looks.

Neutrals

If you plan your wardrobe around some key neutral colors, adding fashion colors whenever you want, you will end up with more combinations of clothes to wear, but fewer items in your wardrobe.

By following the guidelines set out for your coloring characteristics (see pages 62–73), all the colors you choose to wear will work in harmony with each other. Your neutrals will work well with all the colors from your palette, so you will find it easier to base your wardrobe around your neutrals.

Lifestyle choices

Planning that well-coordinated wardrobe means that you need to select which of the neutrals from your palette work best with your lifestyle. If you work in a formal environment, you will need to keep your neutrals on the darker side, which will project more authority. If your lifestyle calls for a more casual and relaxed look, the medium to light neutrals might be your preference as these are more approachable. Of course, changing climate will also influence your choice.

On pages 62–73, we have given each coloring type six basic neutral colors, from the lightest to the darkest. Fashion sometimes dictates what neutrals are available, but they have a much longer lifespan. There will always be whites, beiges, browns, and navies. For some of you, gray will be your black.

Maintaining your wardrobe

Looking after your clothes will ensure they last longer and fall better when you wear them.

- At the end of each wearing, hang your clothes on good hangers (wire hangers are not suitable) and leave them to "breathe" overnight before replacing in your wardrobe.
- Declutter your wardrobe regularly—there is nothing worse than cramming good clothes into an overcrowded wardrobe. They will crease and require more ironing every time.
- Avoid dry-cleaning unless the clothes are really soiled. Manufacturers sometimes specify "dry-clean only," but this is to cover themselves if you don't hand-wash properly. Often, a cool wash will do the trick.
- Avoid hanging heavy knits, which will stretch out. Fold them instead.

RIGHT The muted tone-on-tone colors suit Nina's soft coloring and blend wonderfully with her hair and skin tone.

slimmer look

Looking good

There's no doubt that dressing well makes you feel good! It gives you confidence, and this gives you a positive self-image and esteem. The result is often reflected in improved relationships and work performance.

Finding your look

Looking good is not just a matter of wearing the correct shapes and right colors, it is about completing the look, whether this is wearing the correct-fitting underwear, appropriate shoes for the outfit, or choosing the right glasses.

A single item that doesn't work will distract from the overall look. The following pages look at the details of every item that you might wear in a single day, from your underwear to your makeup. Paying attention to these will make all the difference in creating a slimmer look.

A wardrobe that works for you

Having a workable wardrobe—the right styles and in your color palette—means that whatever the occasion, you should not have to panic and rush out to buy a new head-to-toe outfit, complete with accessories. Once you have found what works for you and suits your lifestyle, you will only be adding to your wardrobe to replace worn-out items, or to update styles.

LEFT Oprah (Deep) is always aware of keeping her look current, without trying to be overly trendy.

RIGHT One of the quickest ways to update your look is to change your hairstyle as Christina Hendricks (Warm) has done here.

Following fashion

We all like to look current and fashionable, whatever our size. Once you have established your basic wardrobe, you can add fashion accents to keep updating your look. This can be anything from a new pair of shoes with the latest heel or an updated purse, or a cardigan in the latest color and length. To show that you are staying trendy, a nail color or hair accessory will do the trick, too. See pages 106–113 for some inspiration on how to put together a complete outfit.

Making time for you

Taking care of your looks with some regular grooming and everyday makeup should never be seen as a chore, rather as part of your daily routine, just as brushing your teeth is. If you can't find time in your schedule, or need some guidance to make the most of your hair and makeup, then take some "me time." A trip to the beauty salon and some time spent with a good hairdresser or a **color me beautiful** image consultant, can show you how to achieve a natural, groomed look quickly and efficiently.

Skin and body care should not be seen as a luxury, but as an essential for all women. Looked after properly, your skin will give you a healthy glow. You'll also avoid the need to cover up imperfections.

Underwear

The correct-fitting underwear will ensure that your clothes fit you properly, giving you a slick and slimmer look. Once you know how to match the right style of bra and underpants to your outfit, you can wear your favorite styles with confidence.

Bras

The size and shape of a woman's breasts changes a number of times throughout her life. This can be due to weight gain or loss, pregnancy, contraception, medication, puberty, menopause, and diet. Whenever you purchase a new bra you should be measured. Be aware that sizes vary between brands, and don't insist on wearing a D, when a DD gives you a better fit. Having your breasts in the right position for what you are wearing is what you need to achieve.

Remember that sometimes your underwear has to be practical—what might be fun and sexy may not give the necessary support during a long day.

RIGHT If you have a color in your palette that your are shy of wearing, why not add it to your underwear selection.

The right bra for:

- **T-shirts** Molded or seamless bras are best, as they give a smooth appearance that will not show through tight-fitting tops.
- **High-neck tops** Full-cut bras (wired or underwired) will give you the perfect support.
- **Deep V-necks** Push-up or plunge bras will give you a perfect cleavage.
- **Wide low-cut tops** Balconette bras will give you uplift and ensure that the straps are placed far enough apart so that they do not show.
- **Strapless tops** Full supporting bras must be worn with your evening wear.

Getting the right fit

Problem	Solution
Bra is loose around the edges	Try a small cup size or adjust the straps
Bra band is riding up your back when you adjust the straps	Try a smaller back size
Bra straps slip off your shoulders	Try a full-cup bra or T-shirt bra
Bra underwiring digs into breast	If the bridge of the bra does not sit flat against the breast-bone, change to a larger cup size
Loose fit	After each wash you may need to readjust the straps

Underpants

You need to achieve a smooth line underneath your clothing with no visible panty line (VPL). Your clothes will always look better if your panties are of a slightly looser fit. Tight panties underneath snug-fitted clothes will make you look bigger, as the elastic around the waist and leg digs in, resulting in an unsightly VPL.

You do not need expert advice or to be measured when buying underpants. However, you do need a selection of different styles to wear under different clothes, but ensure that they give you the coverage, comfort, and support you need.

The right panties for:

- **Pants** Full underpants (à la Bridget Jones) work best underneath pants.
- **Low-waisted skirts or pants** Wear bikini-style panties to avoid revealing the top of your panties above the waist of your skirt or pants.
- **Skirts and dresses** Looser underpants (boy shorts) work well.

SLIMMER STYLE TIPS

When your bra is new, you should fasten it at the loosest end. As it is worn, it will stretch over time and you should tighten it up by moving along the hooks.

Wear special sports bras if you participate in any form of sport, as they are built to protect and support the delicate breast tissue.

Shapewear underwear

Also known as "thigh shapers," "cinchers," and "anti-cellulites," shapewear underwear are designed to help you look slimmer, as they control extra flesh and make the body appear smoother and tighter. You can also get all-in-ones, which give you a totally smooth body line, although these have to be professionally fitted.

Shapewear underwear work by using extra-firm elastic fibers, which simply force unwanted flesh from one area to another. This could result in an unsightly stomach bulge or wobbly thighs. They can also make you feel very warm very quickly, which can be uncomfortable. When considering shapewear underwear, think about whether you really want to feel corseted into these. If you don't have a waist, forcing the creation of one with underwear is not the solution—certainly not in the longer term.

A simple alternative to wearing shapewear underwear is to change the style of the skirt or pants that you want to wear. For minimal control, you can also try more comfortable control panties or control-top panty hose. There are even pants and jeans that come with stomach-control sections.

Petticoats and slips

The popularity of pants has seen the demise of the petticoat. But for a slimmer look, a petticoat or slip worn under an unlined skirt or dress will ensure that it does not cling to your underwear. Modern fabrics mean that static cling has been minimized, making slips more comfortable to wear. Half-length or slips are best worn with skirts or belted dresses.

Underwear color

White, black, and nude are not the only color options, so inject some color, from your color palette (see pages 48–73) into your lingerie and give yourself a feel-good boost right from the beginning of the day.

Hosiery

You can give the illusion of longer, slimmer legs by toning your panty hose or tights with either your hemline or your shoes. A sheen finish will give the illusion of a more shapely calf and ankle, although this is not flattering for very full legs. Instead, opt for opaque panty hose, which always look more slimming. In summer, a lighter denier will be more comfortable. Support panty hose are ideal if you are on your feet all day, and patterned panty hose can be useful for hiding veins. Bright-colored panty hose will draw the eye to the lower part of your body, so you need shapely legs to carry them off.

Nightwear

Do not forget that nightwear—or lounge wear—needs to suit your coloring and style, too. You are at your most vulnerable when you are at home, chilling out, no makeup on, or accessories to enhance your natural look. So make sure that the colors that you choose for these garments are in your palette and that you enjoy wearing them.

RIGHT Be sure that you don't forget to wear the correct colors even when you are relaxing: this will ensure that you look gorgeous even without your makeup on.

The **two piece** floral swimwear that Nina is wearing **flatters her wonderful curves**.

Swimwear

For some, choosing a swimsuit can be stressful—not to mention actually wearing one. By choosing the right style and details, you can feel confident that you can look slimmer on the beach or by the pool.

Finding your style

The thing to remember, when buying a swimsuit, is that it should give you the same kind of support as your underwear, particularly if you are full-busted. You should also consider the basic rules of style when choosing different designs and patterns. Straight bodies look better in geometric patterns, while florals suit curvy body lines.

Getting it right

- If you have straight lines and good shoulders, you will look good in a rectangular, halter or asymmetric neckline.
- Sloping shoulders are better with a slightly wider strap, which grips the shoulder firmly.
- Rounded necklines are good for the more curvy body lines.
- Straight body shapes look good in a one-piece suit with some hip or bust detail. A skimpy bikini that falls low on the hips is good if you feel brave enough to wear one.
- If you have full hips, choose swimwear that has minimal detail over the hip line.

- If you want to have a slimmer-looking stomach, try a swimsuit with a control front panel.
- Most women have great backs, so if you are not confident showing a lot of flesh, but want something different, look for swimwear with low or revealing backs.
- High-cut legs give the illusion of longer legs.
- If you have full thighs, check where the costume finishes on the thigh, as the eye will focus there.
- Straight-cut leg styles really only suit the very long-legged.
- Find companies that sell swimwear as separate pieces if your top and bottom sizes are different.
- Tankinis (bottom + separate top) are a great alternative to a swimsuit or bikini if you want less figure-hugging designs.
- Many brands do matching tops that can be worn over swimsuits, or invest in a sarong or caftan that will cover a multitude of sins.

SLIMMER STYLE TIP
One golden rule before you bare all is to make sure your skin is in tip-top condition and that you use high-factor sun protection.

Footwear

Women simply love fashionable shoes and boots, often giving up comfort for style. However, a well-fitting shoe in a suitable style and height can work with your outfit to give a slimmer look, too.

The right shoes

Poor-fitting footwear can create long-term foot problems and, therefore, you need to ensure that the shoes you wear every day give you the support that you require. You will still fall in love with the most uncomfortable pairs of shoes—just remember to keep them for occasions when you will be sitting down!

Slimmer-looking legs

There are all kinds of tricks to create the illusion of slimmer legs. One way is to make them appear longer. The shoes you wear will make a difference to the appearance of your calves, ankles, and feet.

1 A long toe, whether square or pointed
For a longer leg and narrower ankle.

2 Rounded toes and peeped toes
Shorten the foot. Wear these with a higher heel if you are wearing a skirt.

3 Low-fronted or open shoes
Elongate the leg and slim the ankle.

4 "Toe cleavage"
For a longer foot.

5 High-fronted or lace-up shoes
Best worn with pants or with panty hose in the same color to create a slimming effect.

6 Heeled sandals
Watch where the straps fall: they shouldn't cut the length of your leg.

7 T-bars and straps
Make sure that the color of your panty hose tones with the shoes.

RIGHT A fun pair of shoes can turn an ordinary outfit into something special.

Heel height

The height of the heel you choose is often determined by how comfortable it is to wear. Some consideration, though, should be given to the size of your calf and ankle.

- A very full calf will look unbalanced on a high stiletto heel. A slimming effect is achieved by a heel that is more substantial, which gives the wearer a better-balanced look.
- A low chunky heel on a full leg will not necessarily be flattering. A shaped or wedge-style will produce a slimming effect.
- Wedges are a great way to combine the height of the heel with the comfort and stability of a flat shoe.
- Platforms will always give you extra height; extremely high platforms are a danger!
- Flats and ballet-style shoes, though super comfortable, are not as flattering as a small heel when worn with a skirt.

Boot length

Boots can be as comfortable as you need them to be; or they can be as extravagant as you want. The key rule here for a slimmer-looking leg is to finish the top of the boot at a part of your leg that is narrow.

- A calf-length boot that finishes at mid-calf, the widest point, will draw attention to that part of your leg.
- If the boot finishes at an unflattering part of your leg, ensure that your panty hose are the same color as your boot.

SLIMMER STYLE TIPS

The style of shoe should suit the shape and size of your foot and hold it in place without squeezing it out of shape.

There are specialty boot manufacturers who make boots with different calf widths.

The **scale of your handbag** should **match your scale** in order to achieve a balanced look.

Handbags and purses

The right handbag or purse will make or break your outfit. Get it right and you are the height of elegance, get it wrong and you will disappear in the crowd. With so many styles, colors and textures available, you can never have enough bags!

Handbag style

Handbags and purses are not just a way of carrying your belongings around. You should have a collection of different bags to suit different occasions. If there are colors in your palette that you shy away from wearing, a handbag in that color will work for you and add some fun and interest to your wardrobe.

What your handbag is made of will depend on your budget and lifestyle, and what the bag is used for. Some people love investing in quality leather bags that will last a lifetime, whereas others will buy bags in fabric and have a new one every season.

Remember the golden rule of any purchase: the more you use it, the cheaper the cost per usage!

Getting it right

- The size of a handbag should balance with your scale (see pages 16–17), so, if you are small scale, you need a small-scale bag and so on.
- The shape should complement your clothing lines. A rigid construction is better for straighter lines, while softer, rounded shapes are better on curvier lines.
- Try out handbags, just as you do clothes, checking in a mirror whether the scale, shape, and color work for you.
- Make sure that a handbag is suitable for its purpose. You may be wowed by a great design or color, but if you can't get all your belongings in it, it may not work for you.
- Think about how the bag opens and closes. A bag that you use for traveling should be one that closes completely. If you have young children, how easy is it for them to open the bag and get to the contents?
- Make it easy on yourself to find what you need without having to empty the whole thing out.
- For bags with sections in them, look for one where the linings are light in color.
- Think carefully about bags for occasions. Beautiful leather doesn't look good after a trip to the beach, and a beach bag doesn't really work at a friend's wedding.

SLIMMER STYLE TIP

When you carry your handbag it will fall near your body. So if you have a large bust, carry your handbag at arm's length by your leg or your waist. If you are fuller around the waist and bottom area, avoid handbags dangling at that level and carry them higher up.

Jewelry and accessories

Jewelry, watches, scarves, and belts will help you not only to draw attention away from the parts you do not want to show off, but also to add color and interest to enhance your look and keep you current with the trends.

Finding your style

Following the advice from previous chapters on scale, proportions, and color (see pages 16–19 and 46–75), you can make your outfit a winner for a slimmer you. The larger your scale, the larger the scale of the jewelry and other accessories should be. Small-scale women can make a fashion statement with just one large accessory, though they might prefer smaller pieces for an understated look.

You may have some favorite pieces of fine jewelry that do not necessarily match your scale. If you are large scale, try wearing a few together to create a more balanced look. If your good watch is too small for your scale, wear it with a few bangles to increase the volume.

How to wear scarves

Scarves will add color and new life to any outfit. The choice is virtually limitless, with square or oblong shapes in different sizes and, of course, in different fabrics, too.

- The rules for fabrics and patterns (see pages 42–43) apply here, too.
- A woman with a curvy shape will struggle with a stiff, taffeta scarf or shawl, whereas a soft, chiffon or silk scarf will be more flattering.

- If you have a favorite outfit that is the wrong color, rescue it by wearing the right-color scarf near your face.
- You need to consider where the scarf falls. If you have a short neck, avoid a scarf around your neck and choose a long scarf away from the neck.
- A shawl elegantly draped around the shoulders will hide a multitude of sins, while adding color and interest to the upper body.
- If you have a favorite scarf, but are not sure how to wear it, try using it as a belt or tying it to your handbag for a splash of color.

How to wear belts

The size of your belt will depend on the length of your body and where you need to wear it.

- To lower your waist, a drop belt is ideal.
- If you have a long body, a wider belt will be the best option.

If you want to wear a belt, be aware of the material it is made of.

- If you have a straight body shape, a stiffer belt will be fine for you.
- If you are on the curvy side, your belt should be made of softer material, such as a supple leather.

RIGHT Don't overdo it. Laura's look is just right, with long earrings and a belt. A necklace would be too much with her cowl neckline.

Glasses and sunglasses

For some of you, glasses are a necessity, so make sure they add something stylish to your look; others just love sunglasses and have an ever-expanding collection. Whatever the reason for you wearing glasses, their shapes and colors should enhance your natural look, face shape, and scale. Here again, select a color that is harmonious with your color palette.

Shape of the frame

- Rectangular-shape frames will help to make a full or rounded face look more angular and, therefore, slimmer.
- Rounded or oval shapes work well with rectangular- and angled-face shapes to soften and slim the face.

Weight of the frame

To give yourself the appearance of a smaller face, try a bulkier frame—a fine delicate frame will make your face look bigger.

  If you have a wide nose, a wide, heavy bridge will only bring attention to that part of the face, so make sure you select a style with as narrow and transparent a bridge as you can find. To shorten a long face, choose wider arms to the frame.

Grooming

Looking after your appearance—your hair, skin, nails, and smile–will go a long way to completing your look. Daily beauty routines and regular maintenance will complement your new style and give you the confidence to carry it off.

Hairstyles

One of the first things you, and other people, notice is your hair. Often it will be the easiest and quickest way to give you an instant lift, giving you more confidence and making you look slimmer.

Finding a good hairdresser who will take the time to discuss the various options to suit your lifestyle, face shape, and hair type will pay dividends. Take a picture of a style that you like, or if you see someone with a great haircut that you think might suit you, stop them and ask where they had it done. Most of the time you will find that they are flattered and delighted to share the information with you.

Getting it right

- If you have a high forehead, bangs will help you balance the face. Bangs can be either feathered or straight.
- If you have a prominent nose, you need to balance your hairstyle with some volume at the back of the head.

LEFT Mariah Carey has beautifully groomed hair that is styled around her face to show off her great bone structure.

- Protruding ears are best covered. Avoid tucking hair behind the ears.
- Consider your neck length. Long hair will look great on someone with a long neck; if you have a short or wide neck, your hair needs to be away from your neckline.
- If you have a square jaw, double chin, or jowls, you are best advised to style your hair to finish above or below your chin to avoid drawing attention to that area.
- Always balance the volume of your hair with the size of your head.
- Often, the right products will ensure the cut works for you. Again, your hairdresser can help you with this. Don't forget to ask him or her to teach you how to blow-dry or straighten your hair so that you can achieve a salon look at home.

Using color to flatter you

Color will also play a part in making your hair look good. Using high- or lowlights will give the illusion of volume, which in turn will balance your look better. Your hairdresser is your first port of call to achieve healthy, well-conditioned, and groomed hair.

If your hair is naturally changing color, you may like to refer to *Color Me Younger,* where you will finds tips and advice on how to color your hair most effectively.

Skin care

Do not neglect your basic, daily skincare routine. Keep your skin healthy and younger looking with regular exfoliation and AHA solutions. Treat yourself to the occasional facial at the beauty salon and consider booking eyebrow shaping and tinting, not forgetting your eyelashes—tinted eyelashes are great for regular swimmers, or for going on vacation.

If you tend to have facial hair, there are many options open to you, from bleaching to electrolysis and threading.

Nail care

If you cannot have a regular professional manicure, make time once a week to groom your nails, keeping cuticles at bay, your nails a manageable length, and finishing with a clear polish.

Feet tend to take the brunt of any extra weight you may have and need some regular TLC. A pedicure is wonderful, but if this isn't possible, make sure you look after your feet with at least biweekly sessions to remove dead skin; exfoliate, too, and make sure your toenails are trimmed.

A winning smile

A great smile is an asset, so visit your dentist regularly and at the same time book a hygienist appointment. Teeth whitening does not have to cost a fortune and this is something you may consider doing from time to time to brighten up your smile

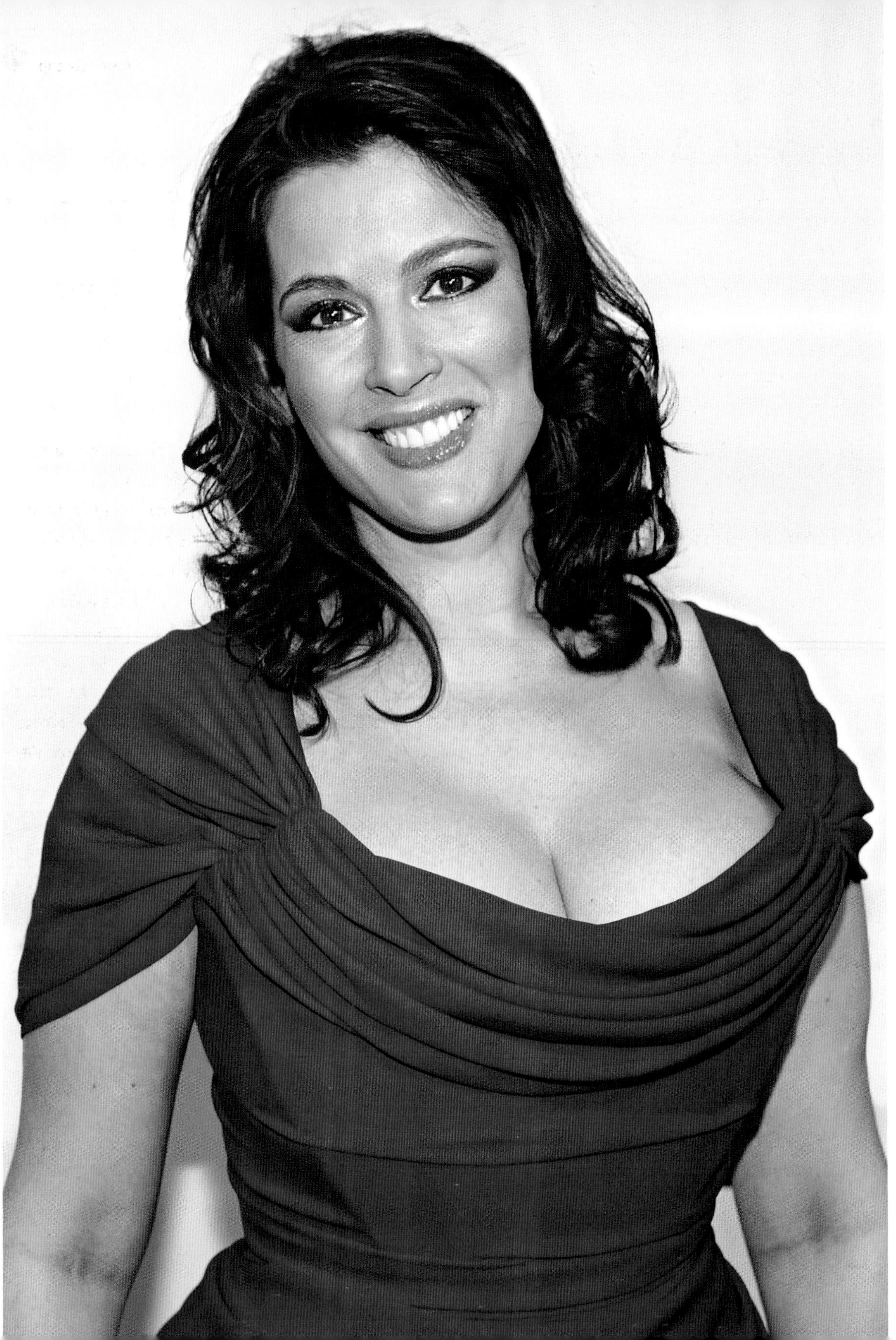

Your makeup

Makeup is not rocket science—it is simply a matter of learning a few tricks and knowing your own face. Applying makeup does not have to take hours; a few basic tips will ensure you are making the most of yourself in minutes.

Makeup colors

Colors need to complement your natural coloring (see pages 98–103) and the clothes you are wearing. Good-quality and clean tools are essential for getting the best from your cosmetics. Always start with a cleaned, toned, and moisturized face.

Sparkling eyes

Applying eye shadows in the correct colors, and mascara, will ensure that your eyes keep on talking to others.

- Mascaras that lengthen and curl the lashes are a great bonus and must-have in your makeup bag.
- Arching your eyebrows will elongate the face and give a slimmer appearance.

Shaping the face

Applying blushers can help to give the illusion of a slimmer face.

- A blusher applied in a straight line and blended along the cheekbones is more flattering than a blob on the apple of your cheek.

- Shaders are a great help in minimizing jowls, strong jaw lines, and double chins.
- Using a large blush brush, brush your blusher along the prominent areas and then apply a highlighter on the chin (or tip of your nose or forehead to bring attention to those areas).
- If you have a prominent or wide forehead, either use your hairstyle to cover it, or apply shader on the side of the forehead to narrow it, or on the top of the forehead by the hairline to shorten it. Don't forget to highlight the middle of your forehead.

Winning smiles

Lip pencils, lipsticks, and lip glosses only take seconds to apply and instantly give energy.

- If you have thin lips, apply a lighter or brighter lipstick and try using a gloss.
- For full lips, darker shades will help to minimize them. Avoid glosses.

LEFT Nigella Lawson's deep coloring is balanced with strong make-up colors.

Light

With your light appearance, the overall look of your makeup needs to be defined, but delicate.

1 EYE PENCIL: Coffee
2 EYE SHADOW: Champagne
3 EYE SHADOW: Fawn
4 EYE SHADOW: Pewter
5 BLUSHER: Marsala

6 LIP PENCIL: Natural
7 LIPSTICK: Dusty rose
8 LIPSTICK: Tulip
9 LIP GLOSS: Dune

SLIMMER STYLE TIP
Your look will be more successful if you avoid wearing black eyeliner and mascara.

Deep

Your strong, dark eyes will come alive with equally dark and strong eyeliners and shadows.

1 EYE PENCIL: Eggplant
2 EYE SHADOW: Mocha
3 EYE SHADOW: Smoke
4 EYE SHADOW: Apricot
5 BLUSHER: Muscat

6 LIP PENCIL: Russet
7 LIPSTICK: Tomato
8 LIPSTICK: Mahogany
9 LIP GLOSS: Sangria

SLIMMER STYLE TIP
You can soften the effect of your lipstick by wearing a lip gloss.

Warm

Your warm coloring needs to be complemented by shades and tones of makeup that are warm and golden.

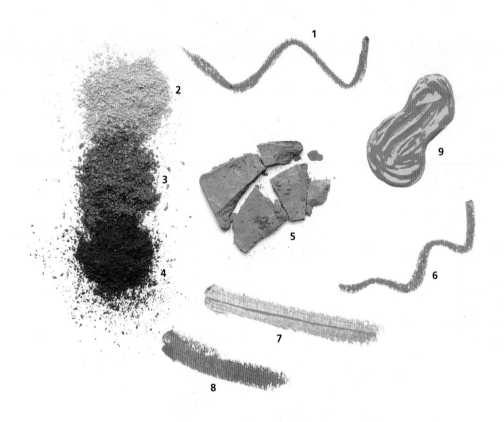

1 EYE PENCIL: Moss
2 EYE SHADOW: Peach
3 EYE SHADOW: Khaki
4 EYE SHADOW: Bay leaf
5 BLUSHER: Almond

6 LIP PENCIL: Spice
7 LIPSTICK: Sheer copper
8 LIPSTICK: Terra cotta
9 LIP GLOSS: Warm sand

SLIMMER STYLE TIP
Mascara is often the make or break for somebody of your coloring.

Cool

Your cool tones are best complemented by blue and lavender, while cool pinks and mauves are best for lipsticks.

1 EYE PENCIL: Granite
2 EYE SHADOW: Opal
3 EYE SHADOW: Lavender bliss
4 EYE SHADOW: Heather
5 BLUSHER: Rose

6 LIP PENCIL: Posie
7 LIPSTICK: Cerise
8 LIPSTICK: Soft mauve
9 LIP GLOSS: Pink shell

SLIMMER STYLE TIP
An eyebrow pencil will be your best friend if your eyebrows lose their color.

Clear

Don't be afraid to go for stunning eye makeup to complement those bright eyes. With softer eyes, try a stronger lipstick.

1 EYE PENCIL: Teal
2 EYE SHADOW: Melon
3 EYE SHADOW: Peppermint
4 EYE SHADOW: Indian ocean
5 BLUSHER: Sienna

6 LIP PENCIL: Cantaloupe
7 LIPSTICK: Strawberry
8 LIPSTICK: Warm pink
9 LIP GLOSS: Mango

SLIMMER STYLE TIP
To give intensity to your lipstick, do not forget to use your lip pencil all over your lips.

Soft

Blending your eye shadows well is important so that the colors do not overpower the gentle tones of your eyes.

1 EYE PENCIL: Coffee
2 EYE SHADOW: Gold whisper
3 EYE SHADOW: Cocoa
4 EYE SHADOW: Steel
5 BLUSHER: Candy

6 LIP PENCIL: Natural
7 LIPSTICK: Sandalwood
8 LIPSTICK: Mulberry
9 LIP GLOSS: Alfresco

SLIMMER STYLE TIP

Do not go out of the house without your lipstick on.

putting it together

Formal office

When you put together a formal work wardrobe, you will need to think about the lines of your body and the clothes you require to ensure a professional and slimming look.

Key pieces

Straight lines
- Fitted jacket with narrow lapels
- Pants with creases
- Straight skirt
- Pleated skirt
- Plain top
- Shift dress
- Handbag
- Shoes

Curvy lines
- Shawl-collar or collarless jacket
- Bias-cut skirt
- Flip skirt
- Full pants
- Wrap top or gathered top
- Princess-line dress
- Soft bucket handbag
- Classic court shoes

shawl-collar jacket

classic court shoes

bias-cut skirt

soft bucket handbag

Casual office

A casual work environment calls for a different wardrobe, while you want it to remain smart and business-like. The rules of grooming still apply.

Key pieces

Straight lines
- Shaped cardigan
- Flat-fronted pants
- Paneled skirt
- Long, straight skirt
- Shirt
- Patterned scarf
- A-line dress
- Saddle handbag
- Boot shoe

Curvy lines
- Long cardigan
- Flared pants
- Wrap skirt
- Full skirt
- Blouse
- Crossover dress
- Drawstring handbag
- Ankle boots

shaped cardigan

patterned scarf

boot shoes

flat-fronted pants

Yummy mommy

If you like fun, colorful, but practical clothes, then our yummy-mommy style gives you the flexibility of a coordinated wardrobe with a lot of different options.

Key pieces

Straight lines

- Straight raincoat
- Pencil skirt
- Shift dress
- Jeans
- Cropped pants
- Twin set
- Cotton shirt
- Hat

Curvy lines

- Belted raincoat
- Bias-cut skirt
- Patterned wrap dress
- Flared denim skirt
- Wide-leg pants
- Long cardigan
- Blouse
- Pumps
- Tote bag

pumps

belted raincoat

tote bag

wide-leg pants

Country

You are the lady who likes order and rules in her wardrobe.
Don't forget to keep reasonably current, though, even if it is
with a new fun pair of rain boots.

Key pieces

Straight lines

- Quilted down vest
- Tartan scarf
- Turtleneck sweater
- Patterned skirt
- Classic pants
- Loafers
- Pearl earrings
- Woolly tights

Curvy lines

- Belted raincoat
- Patterned scarf
- Round-neck sweater
- Paneled tweed skirt
- Soft corduroy belted pants
- Lace-up shoes
- Umbrella
- Opaque tights

classic sweater

pearl earrings

woolly tights

patterned skirt

loafers

Pretty feminine

If you love beautiful fabrics, a lot of details, and looking feminine, here is a selection of clothes that will give you a variety of looks. Don't overaccessorize, however.

floral dress

pretty jewelry

soft handbag

detailed shoes

Key pieces

Straight lines
- Patterned shift
- Blouse with flat ruffle
- Waterfall cardigan
- Flip skirt
- Straight skirt
- Pretty pumps
- Detailed constructed bag

Curvy lines
- Floral dress
- Lacy blouse
- Belted cardigan
- Tiered skirt
- Asymmetric hemline shirt
- Pretty sweater with bows
- Detailed shoes
- Detailed soft handbag

Sporting

There is nothing that you like more than being comfortable and relaxed. A little thought in your purchases will help you to achieve a well-groomed look.

Key pieces

Straight lines

- Slim-fit joggers
- Quilted vest
- Chinos
- Vest top
- Straight short skirt/ woollen tights
- Crew-neck sweater
- Blazer
- Sneakers
- Shoulder bag

Curvy lines

- Wide-leg joggers
- Shaped fleece
- Stretch jeans
- T-shirt
- Soft denim dress
- Cowl-neck sweater
- Hoodie
- Sneakers

quilted vest

sneakers

chinos

shoulder bag

Global

Your wardrobe will be eclectic and unrelated. Remember, keep to the same group of colors if you are mixing patterns and textures together.

Key pieces

Straight lines
- Long, straight skirt
- Straight jeans
- Folky, long scarf
- Unusual hat
- Mock-fur coat
- Long, sleeveless textured cardigan
- Boots
- Basket

Curvy lines
- Full skirt
- Flared pants
- Patterned wrap
- Fun, rounded hat
- Tapestry bag
- Long, sleeveless, textured cardigan, belted
- Sandals
- Folky jewelry

long, sleeveless cardigan

folky jewelry

tapestry bag

gathered top

full skirt

sandals

Glamour

There will always be that special occasion when you want to stand out and be noticed. The key to a successful look is not to lose sight of your shape or coloring.

Key pieces

Straight lines

- Evening coat
- Full-length shift dress
- Stunning, shaped jacket
- Draped A-line dress
- Daytime sparkling sleeveless top
- Straight-cropped silk pants
- Evening bag
- Heels

Curvy lines

- Velvet cape
- Bias-cut dress or ball gown
- Beautiful wrap
- Chiffon draped crossover dress
- Drapy top
- Silk palazzo pants
- Evening purse
- Heels

silk, draped A-line dress

glittering jewelry

colorful purse

killer heels

case
studies

Lisa: Petite

An awareness of your body shape is essential in dressing for a slimmer look. Even if you are considered short, you can learn to give the illusion of being slimmer by dressing in such a way that you look taller. It's all a matter of understanding your best features and how to dress them.

Our model

Lisa, our Deep model, is not particularly tall; she has a short neck, and not very long arms. She is proportionally longer in the body, which means she is also slightly shorter in the legs.

Getting it wrong

- The high neckline of Lisa's jacket emphasizes her short neck.
- The double-breasted jacket makes her bust look very full.
- The belted waist gives Lisa the appearance of being short-waisted (which she isn't).
- The fabric of the jacket is far too crisp for her soft curves.
- The short skirt appears to cut her legs, making her legs look wider.
- The ankle straps of Lisa's shoes make her legs look much wider than they actually are.

PETITE STYLE TIP
Avoid color blocking and banding as this will make your appear shorter and, therefore, wider.

Getting it right

- The dress is made of soft jersey knit, which glides over Lisa's curves, making her look slimmer; it gives her an elongated look rather than the appearance of being cut into sections.
- The open neckline reveals a beautiful neck and chest area.
- The three-quarter-length sleeves flatter her arms and wrists .
- The crossover line of the top of the dress accommodates her full bust.
- The deep waistband balances her torso.
- The open-front, pointed-toe shoes finish her look by flattering her legs and ankles.

Christie: Tall

Tall women often need to consider scale and proportion when putting a wardrobe together, and it can be a case of mixing and matching different styles of clothing. It can be difficult to achieve a feminine look that works: be wary that the latest fashion might not necessarily be right for you.

Our model

Christie has Deep coloring. She is wonderfully tall and full-figured. She has a large-scale bone structure, long arms and legs, and a full bust. Her neck is quite short for her height and her shoulders slope down from her neck.

Getting it wrong

- Although the charcoal is a good color for Christie, wearing one color from head to toe emphasizes her height.
- The slash neckline of the dress does not flatter her short neck.
- The high neckline makes Christie's bust look higher and fuller.
- The cap sleeves give the illusion that Christie has very long arms.
- The jewelry Christie is wearing is far too small for her scale.

TALL STYLE TIP
Mixing plain and patterned pieces can help to break up your appearance.

Getting it right

- The colorful, boldly patterned, A-line top balances Christie's height and scale.
- The open neckline and detailing under the bust draw attention away from the fullest part of Christie's chest, making it now appear to be in the right place.
- The band around the hemline of the top adds interest to the look and makes Christie appear perfectly balanced in height and scale.
- The three-quarter-length sleeves are softly gathered at the shoulder line for a far more flattering look.
- The teal top, with its striking pattern, suits Christie's Deep coloring perfectly.
- Dark-brown pants help to minimize Christie's full hips.

Emma: Straight

Understanding the basic outline of your body will guide you in choosing the designs and clothing lines that are most likely to flatter you. An important consideration for a woman with a straight figure is to have a good idea as to the types of fabric she can wear.

Our model

Emma has the straightest body line of all our models. She is 5 feet 9 inches tall and her top half is slightly larger than her bottom half. She has no real waist definition.

Getting it wrong

- The heavyweight, deconstructed jacket overwhelms Emma, giving a bulky, cluttered look to her silhouette.
- The soft shoulder line gives the appearance that she has bad posture.
- The belt makes Emma's waist look broad.
- The belt gathers around Emma's hips and bottom, making them look much larger than they actually are.
- Wearing the same color in both the jacket and pants emphasizes Emma's height, even though the color suits her deep coloring.
- The full volume of the sleeves hides Emma's silhouette, making her arms look full and wide.

Getting it right

- Because Emma is tall she can afford to color-block her clothes.
- Colorful tights add a glamorous appeal to her look.
- The shift-style dress suits and flatters Emma's straight lines.
- The vest gives her a good, straight shoulder line.
- The vest ends at a narrow point on Emma's hips, giving the illusion of them being slightly wider, so balancing her look.
- The narrow belt worn under the vest gives the appearance of a waist that isn't really there.
- Overall, Emma looks as if she has dropped pounds, just by changing the fabric and style of her clothes.

STRAIGHT STYLE TIP
Wear clothes that give the illusion of a waist and keep clothing lines straight.

Sarah: Curvy

Women who have a lovely, fuller figured, curvy body line are sometimes tempted to hide behind their clothes rather than show their curves to their advantage. It is possible to achieve a glamorous, slimmer look with the right styles and types of fabric and accessories.

Our model

Sarah is one our wonderfully full-figured, curvy models. She has a lovely full bust, a slim, well-defined waist, and curvy hips and thighs.

Getting it wrong

- The shirt is an unsuitable garment for a large bust; traditionally worn by men, it tends not be designed for a full chest.
- The shirt pulls in all directions because the fabric is very stiff.
- Sarah is unable to fasten the shirt over her bust.
- The shirt finishes at the widest point on Sarah's hips, making them look wider than they actually are.
- The shift dress is made from a crisp fabric and looks wide below the waistline.
- The ankle straps and low heels of Sarah's shoes make her legs appear shorter than they are.

CURVY STYLE TIP
Don't be afraid of showing off your curves in a soft, flattering fabric.

Getting it right

- The soft, knitted dress shows off Sarah's curvy body to maximum effect.
- She looks slimmer and taller wearing just one color.
- The detail in the middle of the dress shows off Sarah's small waist.
- The higher heel and slight platform of the shoes help to elongate her legs.
- This style of shoe enhances Sarah's wonderful ankles and calves.
- Overall, Sarah achieves the illusion of losing inches, just by dressing differently.

Mel: Large scale

Whatever your shape, you will also need to work out your bone structure as this dictates whether you are small, average, or large scale. The patterns you wear should balance with your scale: small pattern on small scale, large pattern on larger scale.

Our model

Mel has beautiful Light coloring. Scale and proportion are important for her, as she has a larger bone structure, and her hips are fuller than the top half of her body.

Getting it wrong

- The small, tiny, delicate pattern of Mel's blouse does not work with her larger bone structure.
- The tiny ruffle down the front of the blouse is lost in the details of the pattern.
- The light, cropped pants draw the eye to the lower half of Mel's body, which is not flattering.
- The fabric of the cropped pants is fairly crisp, and Mel will always look better in slightly softer and more fluid fabric below the waist.

Getting it right

- Mel has light coloring and can wear darker colors on her lower half; these help to minimize her slightly fuller hips and thighs.
- The big, bold pattern of the colorful blouse works with Mel's bone structure.
- The blouse brings the attention to the top half of Mel's body.
- The top finishes above the widest point on Mel's hips, making them look slimmer.
- The narrow ribbon belt, worn lower, shows off Mel's waist and gives her shape.

LARGE SCALE STYLE TIP

Think about the details of your clothes and make sure they balance with your scale.

Index

Acknowledgments

An awful lot of people are involved in producing a book, and this one certainly benefited from the input, hard work, and contribution of many talented and energetic women. They are: Helen Boyle, Clare Churly, Vanessa Davies, Katy Denny, Mel Halaçoglu, Lisa John, Zoe Lem, Christie Pidgley, Anna Southgate, Penny Stock, and last but not least Fiona Wellins. Special thanks to all our lovely models who disrobed, during what has been one of the coldest winters in history, in beautiful old, but cold, houses. And finally thank-you to everyone else behind the scene at **colour me beautiful** and Hamlyn for their continued support and enthusiasm.

With all our thanks and love to each other, too.

Pat Henshaw and Veronique Henderson

For more information on services, products, and how to become a consultant, contact:
colour me beautiful
Headquarters, Europe, Africa and Middle-East
www.colourmebeautiful.co.uk
t: +44 (0)20 7627 5211
e: info@cmb.co.uk

Clothes and accessories:
LK Bennett: www.lkbennett.co.uk
Sahara: www.saharalondon.com
Spirito di Artigiano: www.artigiano.co.uk
Wall: www.wall-london.com
Spirit of the Andes: www.spiritoftheandes.co.uk

Executive Editor: Katy Denny
Senior Editor: Lisa John
Executive Art Editor: Penny Stock
Designer: Beverly Price
Senior Production Controller: Amanda Mackie
Picture Researchers: Jennifer Veal and Zoë Spilberg
Special Photograpy: © Octopus Publishing Group/Vanessa Davies
Stylist: Helen Boyle

Other Photography: Alamy/D. Hurst 88 top right; /Image Register 096 88 center right below; /Gordon Saunders 88 center left above. Fotolia/Phattman 88 center left below. Getty Images/Larry Busacca 7 bottom left; /Alex Cao 88 top left; /Jemal Countess 21; /Image Source 85; /Matthew Peyton 47 right; /Alexander Tamargo 96; /WireImage 94. Photoshot/Everett 7 top left. Press Association Images/Pablo Martinez Monsivais/AP 20; /Mark J. Terrill/AP 7 right. Rex Features/Christian Lapid 47 left; /Sipa Press 80; /Stewart Cook 81.